CIVIC DUTY

Cover art by Joel Amat Güell
Text Illustrations by Crystal Stone and Ally Frame

Acknowledgements

Thanks to the editors of the following journals in which these poems originally appeared, often in earlier forms:

- Pandemic Isolation, Day 2 in *Across the Social Distances*
- Self Portrait with Quarantine Instructions in *Back Channels*
- Musical Interlude I in *Headline Poetry Review*

Thanks also to Iowa Public Radio for letting me read "Pandemic Isolation, Day 6" and "Pandemic Isolation, Day 14" on air for the *River to River* program on May 8th.

Self Portrait as an American Woman Doll

Her nose isn't a straight line. The eyes
aren't quite level—the left eye bigger.
At the right angle, you can't tell.
At the wrong angle, wrinkles appear
as social distancing lines businesses make
to keep people apart or the lines on the streets
Vegas made for their homeless, too.

She auctions her book for food banks
in different cities, applies for jobs three hours
every day, isolates with a friend, practices
smiling. She walks four miles to call friends
who are alone. She watches new shows
set in other eras every week. Her shoes are wet
with rain, not tears. She only texts her ex to say sorry.

Caucus Accessories

O

ponytail holder

pen

cellphone

water bottle

snacks

name tag

winter jacket

*

My country tis of thee

        -se sticker name-tag interruptions,

of citizen strangers,

        of the right to concealed carry

entitlement religion virus.

        We the people of wasted time.

Sweet land of labor, libel,

        injustice for all. My country

tis of thee-se phantom militia

        viral race to bare faces in public.

Electoral college of miscounted

        votes. moderate

losses. Land of the free

        to lick the Walmart shelves.

the free to be fired. Land of

        the lawless brave. We the sold out

people, we the indulgent

        prayerless feasts.

*

Last Iowa Caucus

Once opened, the wine is a glassy rose
in our cups. We cheer politely
next to the dying dog. He labors
to breathe, like my own dog
the day her stomach filled
with blood like a patched and swollen moon.
The moon doesn't make it dark, my friend
tells her child when the child's eyes saucer
into planetary questions. We'd been
orbiting the food, the words, the songs.
A friend heads to the piano to play
the grief we're all avoiding. Another reads
tarot cards, tells us what we need to hear.
Outside, next to the lake, mice and rabbit
tracks are not parallel lines. I wonder
who started the chase, or if they were
friends meeting for the first time.
Will we cross over politely? The geese
and swans share the open water, the icy
beach. On the other side of the bridge,
a man corkscrews the ice open.
The splinters on the surface extend—
fingers of an open palm
waiting to be read, held.

Jury Duty Accessories

notepad

pencil

binder of
evidence

necklace

video of
evidence

professional dress

Civic Duty

During juror selection,
the defendants' lawyer tells us
his wife broke her collarbone
trying on a dress

and the tragedy of being
mayor in a town
just before four tornados demolished
landmarks & businesses. *The scales of justice*

outside the courtroom
were replaced by hub caps. I notice
the subtle irony of his placement
defending the driver of a motor vehicle

collision with a pedestrian. *Look out*
the window, there's the jail!
we're told as we walk into the room
we can't leave until we all agree

what the young man should pay
for the older man's loss. We speculate
about natural aging, about ourselves, laugh
at the closing statement of the defendant's lawyer

because he tells us how he met his wife,
their philosophy on simplicity, the grandbaby
he'll meet for the first time tomorrow
when we go back to being strangers again,

as if we all never met.
We calculate life
expectancy of the plaintiff:
a 73- year-old man hunched over—

not from the accident—but from life
with scoliosis and arthritic bones. We talk about teeth
at lunch, avoid soda, anxious to be judged
by the dentist in the room. The mechanic

tells us he's also been hit by a car at 10 mph
before, too—it just bruised his thighs.
We spend hours determining formulas
to quantify damage, what we're all losing

daily and what a collision
might have changed. All of the medical
reports have typos from young scribes,
entry-level professionals who don't understand

the potential future losses that could come
from their errors.   Like us.
                    We're told to be
impartial, to avoid empathy, to look only

at the facts presented, to use common
sense as if this was a natural thing:
to place a value on each year
of our fading lives.

Dear ~~Juror~~ Citizen,

Thank you for meeting the civic obligation

hope your experience was a pleasant one

the lawyers seek permission   feedback

Please feel free

respond anonymously if you wish

it will not be used in any way

*CONFIDENTIAL SURVEY IS ENCLOSED

*

America the beautiful
                    jury

tea party embargo
                fruited California wines,

O beautiful for
                        shining sea gains

        made-in-the-USA dustbowl clouds

O beautiful for
                spacious lies,   for amber

ammo sales, for purple
                    heart mountains

amnesty, God shed
                his tears on thee

*

Postcard: Isolation Walk in Wompatuck State Park Before Closures

Quarantine Week 1 Accessories

toilet paper

wine glass

steak/
meat

hand
sanitizer

vape

Pandemic Isolation, Day 2

Life has that new car smell. My dreams
lion with anxiety—loud. *There are spiders*
in Japan, too, I say in my sleep
and what I mean is there's nowhere
to escape the fears. I'm scared
to write poems, to speak all that's terrible
into permanence. Isn't that what poetry does:
manifest? I've conjured love as snowy debris,
hoped the rest would melt. A revised painting:
where the walls become birds, trees. A man

online tells me *Think of ammo as freedom seeds*
when all the stores are sold out. Walking outside,
I almost forget the virus threatens to end so many:
traffic saturating the breeze, children still
playing hockey on their rollerblades. The sun
ignoring the clouds, the urgency. Dogs happy
their owners are always home now. A blue
house on the corner littered with statues: the head
of a Roman man looking indoors. The Italian
warning of what's to come. License

plates read: Massachusetts, the Spirit of America.
A woman tells me, *Martial law. We won't stand*
for that. A man tells me, *Got lead, get fed.*
They'll save us all when everything collapses. I don't
know what it'll look like when it's all over:
the clear Venice canals without boat travel,
the China air without factory smoke, the purple
mountains, amber waves of grain saying hello once again
to the wolves, coyotes, mountain lions. All the insects
that used to hit our windshield when we traveled come back.

Crepe Recipe, Add-ins Vary

Suggested add-ins: yogurt, berries, nuts, bananas, nutella, peanut butter, butter, syrup, confectioners' sugar, mozzarella cheese, tomatoes, basil, sweet potatoes, brussels sprouts, whatever fresh food left in your fridge that might be going bad.

Ingredients:

1 cup all-purpose flour
2 eggs
½ cup water
½ cup milk
¼ teaspoon salt
2 teaspoons melted butter

Whisk flour and eggs like commitments. Add in milk slowly, stir the family. Add salt and butter. Beat hobbies with a spoon. Heat wait-oiled pan. Pour batter. Tilt in a firework circular motion so it's coated evenly. Cook for about two minutes, until the bottom is light brown. Flip expectations. Serve responsibility.

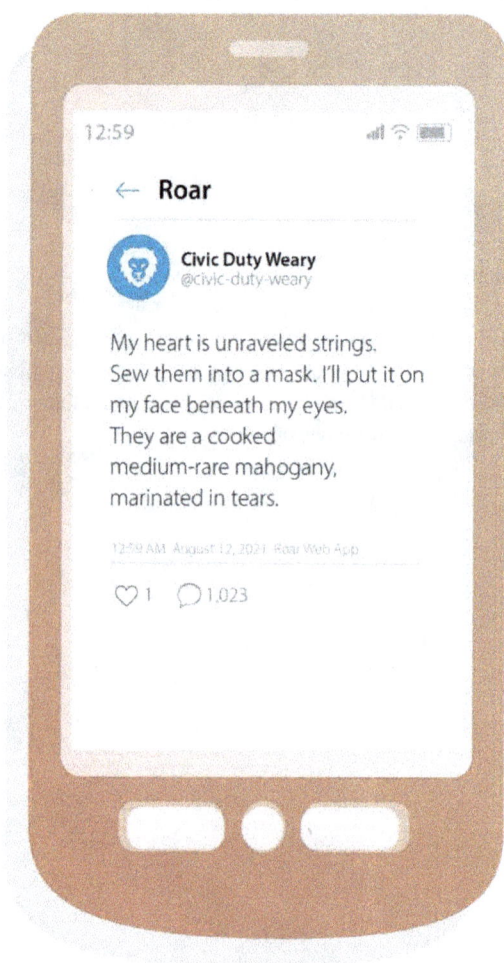

← Roar

Civic Duty Weary
@civic-duty-weary

My heart is unraveled strings.
Sew them into a mask. I'll put it on
my face beneath my eyes.
They are a cooked
medium-rare mahogany,
marinated in tears.

12:59 AM August 12, 2021 Roar Web App

♡ 1   💬 1,023

Pandemic Isolation, Day 6

Driving past the graffiti rocks on the highway back
I still hear the boy on his scooter
bouncing down the path yelling,
"It's not smooth! It's not smooth! You told me
it would be smooth!" But no one lied to me.
It's been mostly silent. On my walk,
even the birds in the woods paused,
closed to mating calls. The mossy eyes
of the rocks gloved shut. Swans bathe noiselessly

in the mist. On the ground paprika-ed
in pine needles & cayenne leaves, I find
two tombstones: one buried by a tree, engraved,
but illegible. The second bitten down, tangled
in the tree's roots. Did the dead bodies
silently instruct the tree to grow? I grab on
to a rope, walk over a bridge
made only of small branches, partial plywood
planks, gathered like a beaver's dam.

I soak my feet in muddy puddles, unbalanced,
unprepared for the walk, the way everything
changes. Another uprooted tombstone interrupts the end
of my walk, but this time completely legible,
seemingly new. How close are we all to our fears, the life
we've been avoiding for years.
In less than a week, everything on the edge:
a singular, stranded stone.

Quarantine Upper Body Routine

Strength (4-5 sets)
Bicep curls (10 reps)*
Shoulder presses (10 reps)*

Superset (3 sets)
Push ups (10 reps)
Tricep dips (10 reps)
Lateral & ventral raises (10 reps) *

HITT (30 seconds on, 10 seconds off)
Mountain climbers (x3)
Squat jumps (x3)
Jumping jacks (x3)

*sub in household items if weights are unavailable; i.e., paint cans, laundry detergent, dish soap, flour or rice bags, large bottles of alcohol or chicken broth, old textbooks you can no longer donate or safely mail, your younger siblings, elderly parents, or partner

Pandemic Isolation, Day 14

When a job rejects me kindly, my friend
says reading the email is like *eating flowers.* Good,
but not good enough. I'm walking alone, trying
to enjoy the floral taste of sunlight, the sparkling
scent of bay, the windy touch of grass, rocky breath
of sand. A man walks by the stone I rest on and sits
20 ft further on the hill, on top of his skateboard.

I am a stranger in my own country. I no longer know
how to navigate the basics: laundry, shopping, cooking,
teaching. The virus is author and translator of two tongues
I've never learned. The park has a warning
that has nothing to do with corona. Enter at your own risk:
COYOTES. I've never seen one, just turkeys fighting
cars that try to park, fanning feathers, gobbling blues.

2:02

← **Roar**

Civic Duty Weary
@civic-duty-weary

Home is where my love is. Social
distanced from heart.
#loveisnottourism #travelban
#heartbreak

2:02 PM October 6, 2020 Roar Web App

♡ 199 💬 57

Week 2 Quarantine Accessories

resume

pasta

netflix

vodka

Recipe with Shelf Stable Pantry Food

2 cans of tuna, drained
2 cans of cream of mushroom soup
1 can of peas (if any)
1 can of black olives
½ cup of shredded cheese
1 lb of pasta, whatever shape is left

Boil water on the stove. Pre-heat oven to 375°. Cook pasta at the lowest time so it stays *al dente*. While pasta boils, add the other ingredients into the bowl. Drain pasta. Add to bowl. Stir well. Place ingredients in a casserole dish with breadcrumbs and cheese. Bake for 15 minutes or until top has browned. Serve.

Quarantine Lower Body Routine

Strength (4-5 sets)
Squats (@ 30 lbs per hand, 10 reps)
Deadlifts (@ 30 lbs per hand, 10 reps)

Superset (3 sets)
Lunges (10 reps)
Curtsy Lunges (10 reps)
Side Leg Raises (10 reps per side)

HITT (30 seconds on, 10 seconds off)
Burpees (x3)
Lateral side jumps (x3)
Plank hold (x3)

Pandemic Isolation, Day 17

We're washing our conversations
in the bathtub, wearing them like clothes.
The laundromat services are too
risky. Our words are starting to feel

stiff, have a lingering odor.
We order groceries
online, make recipes without
all their ingredients:

korma without ginger,
mushroom risotto without mushrooms,
corn chowder without corn,
tuna casserole without peas. Before this,

I imagined a teeth cleaning, an eye
appointment and my annual pap
before May graduation. I have health
care dreams of unemployment checks

I didn't earn enough to receive.
What stops first—quarantine
or the care I can afford to receive?
At home, I see videos of local

teachers driving around the neighborhood
with signs about missing their students.
Gloved flirting leaves boxed presents
at the door. They always come

later than people need. I apologize
to everything, miss it all and nothing:
a breath of fresh air wrung out, happy hour
priced in-person smiles, bad date dresses,

beer cozy humidity hair,
cowboys at karaoke, grocery store
shopping. We American hero

the laundromats, post offices, hospitals,

teachers at homes, look the other way
from pastors hosting maskless
churches, men bringing machine
guns to the closed offices.

star spangled banner

                deaths, for the opening

economy

        O say   can you

see

        broad stripes and bright star

                        lunchable secrets

star spangled banner

           terrorism sprinkling

protests

           over the nintendo

year of the Netflix

              home of the switch

*

Pandemic Isolation, Day 21

My friend thinks *Tiger King* is fiction, but I've met people
like them before: a pawn shop owner in Cleveland,
Mississippi with a taste for captivity—
ringed tailed lemurs in a cage by the door.

An Iowa farmer in line beside me at a comedy show
who whispered that she raises skunks, raccoons,
and ferrets to sell as pets to buyers worldwide.
When another friend messages me

that she's so ill she can barely move,
we worry she has coronavirus. I wonder
what will happen to her, to the others
who've died alone, from coronavirus, suicide,

or natural aging in isolation. Most of our families are
states away: we send flowers to say *I love you,*
or *thank you,* even though they can't touch the bouquet for 72 hours.
My friend is so nervous about contracting corona,

he takes his clothes off at the door after work
in front of my recording webcam. I laugh so hard
that my professor tells me I can turn it off.
So when I'm asked if *Tiger King* is an important cultural moment,

I want to say no, it's boring, but it brings so many of us
outside the virus. A man on the virtual open mic
uses a tropical island backdrop, then mountains of China.
Maybe next week he'll dress up as Joe, make it a zoo.

Week 3 Accessories

laundry detergent

face mask

dish
soap

wifi

gloves

Postcard: Lockdown Views from the Living Room

Quarantine Full-Body Routine

Strength (4-5 reps)
Walk to the kitchen (x10)
Wash the packages (x10)
Oversleep (x10)
Turn off the news (x10)

Superset (3 sets)
Check Twitter (x10)
Check Facebook (x10)
Check Instagram (x10)

HIIT (30 sec, 10 sec off)
Cry (x3)
Feel guilty (x3)
Swipe right (x3)

Pandemic Isolation, Day 26

Bird houses fastened
to trees growing
in the middle of a flooded
valley. A shed graffitied
with a smiling emoji. Mowed
grass beside a sign: *Wildflower meadow.*
DO NOT MOW. There's so much evidence
of life to witness every time outdoors.
Another sign reads: Alpaca poo, $5.
In the woods, an empty eagle nest,
a beaver dam we use as a bridge.

A boy passing on his bike asks, *Did you see*
a dead hiker on the trail? His mom says,
Ignore him. Teenagers. But I look, passing
by the cranberry bogs on the way
home with colors that resemble
burned or buried bridges.
We're indoors for the imminent
death we haven't all yet seen.
Like the mowed wildflowers,
death hasn't yet greeted us
personally, surfaced.

← **Roar**

Civic Duty Weary
@civic-duty-weary

I'm having grad school FOMO. But I also have home renovation FOMO, retirement account FOMO, travel FOMO, beauty trend FOMO, kitchen appliance FOMO, romance FOMO, and how do y'all decide what you want to do with your time?

4:34 PM May 17, 2022 Roar Web App

♡ 678   💬 579

II

Election Eve

When asked to flip the tofu,
I switch the music, change

the moon. He opens the lid
and steam doesn't devour the night.

This is what it means to have.
I take a spatula to the bottom

of the pan, finish what's left.
What's left unfinished around us:

Not the poker table. Not the deck,
or the woodburning stove. He stuffs

the mouth of the open bottle
with a paper towel cork

to keep it fresh. The missing
glass of the door frame is only

a harmless, aged mistake. So easy
to walk through, or forget.

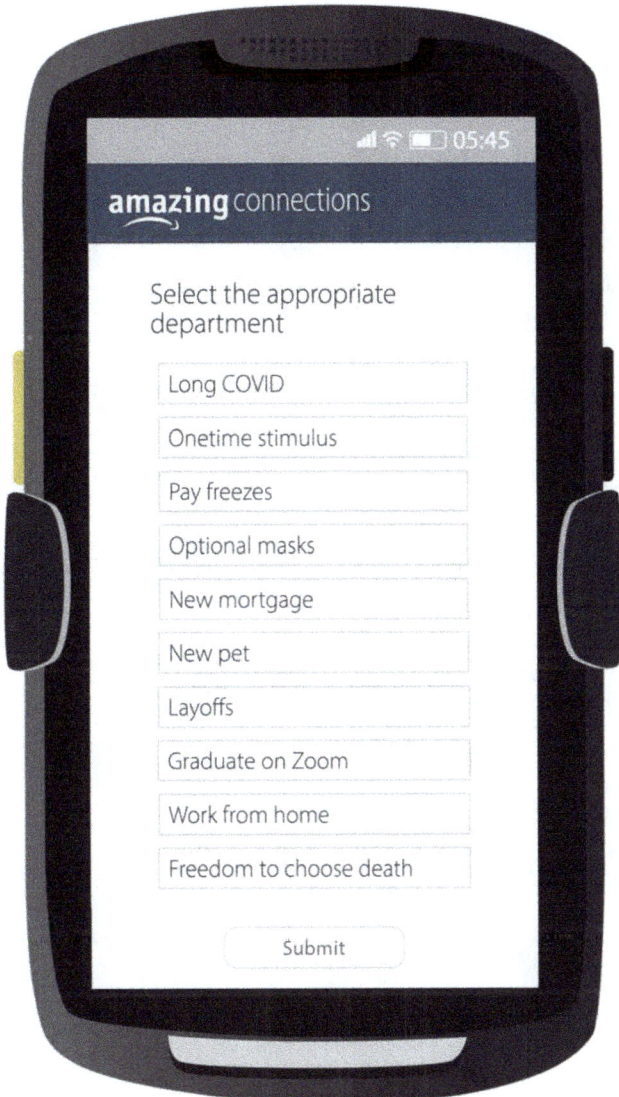

amazing connections

05:45

Select the appropriate department

Long COVID

Onetime stimulus

Pay freezes

Optional masks

New mortgage

New pet

Layoffs

Graduate on Zoom

Work from home

Freedom to choose death

Submit

Puerto Rico Dreaming Alone with COVID

We made coquitos and sat
in the hot tub to summer

our Christmas with wet,
hot dreams. My hair was a beachy

sand. His eyes were a wavy
blue. *Die Hard* played

in the background. I got sick
to the sound of glass shattering.

I woke up with a fever
I shared. We quarantined

alone. Something changed after.
His eyes sobered a ring

of still water. His skin
eroded joy, taste, smell.

Love has always been a version
of loneliness. Temporary color

that comes out after the daily
wash. He was a day

trader, committed to selling.
I've always preferred a more natural

look, a serious long-term investment.
Our last meal together was comfort

food, secrets, and tears. We became
strangers, friends, and strangers again.

New House Accessories

new home

Keys

43

Depression

It's a sickness, this need
for bed. Like a fever dream,
in and out of color. I'm paling. The night
sweats leave leaf-prints
on the sheets. My body concrete
between the seasons.
I'm learning the texture
of silence. The way that years
of damages are covered
with a fresh coat of paint.
Beside me, my dog naps,
wags her tail as she dreams.
She barks a word
that sounds a lot like go.
I'm imagining this, too: a whole life
without patched up walls,
missing gutters, paint peeling
from the closet racks.

Anxiety

The smoke is jeweled air. I breathe
in so my lungs will set the stone
in the ring of my internal state.
Concealed carry
gem. Won't break
the heartbrain barrier.
"You're not bad, but you don't
have to be good." I'm misremembering
a poem in my father's voice.
The gem blinks instead of sparkles
in the light of the truth. I'm breaking
all the rules, here in bed past
the tarnished sunrise
full of clouds. My dog is oblivious
because I'm living
like a dog. With kibbles
of hope today, a gentle
bite at the thinning air.

Unemployment Accessories

dog bed

CHIPS
BEANS

comfy
clothes

prescriptions

Unemployment

It's been a pledge-of-allegiance
morning, one nation
under adderall, prozac,
zyprexa, hydroxine, loryna,
caffeine, THC, hemp oil.
Teeth brushed in charcoal.
Dog walked at the usual park.
The religion of routine
that I'm throwing away.
I'm tired of my own needs.
My dog jumps out the window
when I stop the car
trying to follow me. I don't blame her.
We're all trying to get out.
She's a heavy sigh away
from an unhooked leash,
but I'll always wear a collar,
blue or white, looking out.
My choices are a cloudy sky.
My heart is cumulous strand.

Party in the ~~Post-Colonial~~ USA

Plane delay in T-U-L

               with a negative COVID test

welcome to the land

                of poor access

not worried about fitting in

                jumped in the cabin for the first time

in years, asking people

                wear their tests and masks at.

This is all so crazy,

                everybody seems so unphased.

Amazon Accessories

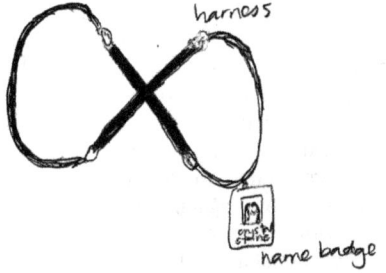

harness

name badge

Steel toed
sneakers

gloves

box
cutter

First Days at Amazon Haibun

We didn't need a resume—just an ID, a clean drug test, a timely clock in, a silent phone in our pockets. Before the dress code, they warned us about active shooters. "If you choose to fight, you need to go all in." The training was non-verbal animation and unfamiliar terms. My trainer was new. He wore a black durag and blue sweatpants tucked into his cowboy boots. Another asked me, "What are you, five?" when he saw my harness tangled. A peer avoided my gaze at the 4 am shift. I folded gaylords and looked for water spiders to wrap the pallets. Every time they were completed, a different trainer would show us a new way to stack the boxes. We redid the same pallet over and over again. I practiced the distance I could scan the laser. The laser saw the spectrum of expressions the shift held. What surprised me most wasn't the chaos, but how normal it was. Our shift was

empty time, unneeded
breaks, stories about safety
featuring bloody trails.

4 am Shift

Most of life is waiting:
for your nails to grow in, your roots
to grow out, the degree, the wedding,
the next step, the moment
when the packages come in. It's boring,
this returning. Like vacation week spent
in your hometown with dusty
friendships. Where does the time
go? It's hard to tell between the umami
scent of fluorescent rays from the metallic
roller suns. They don't stop for dawn
or dusk. They are their own horizon.
Packages of time crinkle at the speed.

Trinity of the Working Class
after Sheila Dong

Chutes & ladders is missing a jam pole. Black gloves. The steel whistles of holiday cheer. Footprints and stickers on the veil of the chutes. Everyone smiles. The players are cardboard

packages. Wedged in a palette. Squeeze damaged. Unopened. Who will be delivered home first? Say cheese for the scanner. Chutes & ladders wants to be

the blue collar cousin of Candyland, but it's too happy. It doesn't chain smoke on fifteens. Candyland is a starving artist. There are no leftovers to sneak from a corporate fridge. They change their hair quarterly, but not in sync with the seasons. The town is bubble wrapped with chance. An extra warehouse shift. Home is a rolling, screeching stop

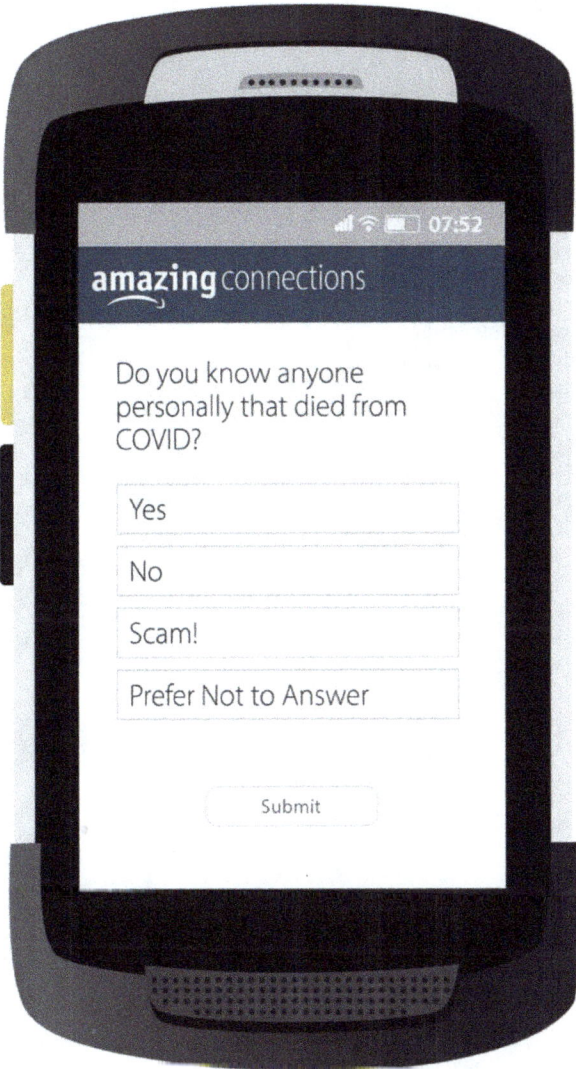

Ripley's! Believe It or Not

Gandhi was a Libra. Every
billionaire has an ugly

sweater. They don't like cats,
but tolerate them. We tolerate

billionaires too because they run
the city. We don't have a choice.

The incense smoke is shaped like
the mice my dogs don't care

to chase. They taste each other's food,
instead, just to discover what they might be

missing. Sometimes we think we do,
but we don't know how to get what we need.

Settling

Saturday has the sweet tooth urge
to be decadent, but the pies went moldy
so quickly. Breakfast is canned hash.
The sky drags the sun by its frizzy
rays. Who cares that the day
has finally warmed
into winter, the grass slipped
into crystalline shoes. The dog puts
her paw over my lips when she wants
to be held. Everyone I know waits
for a good job, but I'm satisfied with any.
What I have to offer is only a few
raspy questions. My life is the crawl
space under the house. The day
has cobwebs. The night has no
iridescent spin or shine.

My Dog Looks Out the Window at the Sunset

and my friend laughs, tells me no,
dogs are colorblind. They don't

notice the vibrant shifts
the way we do. The supply chain

clouds break like the day
and here we are, only looking

at the colors. The supermarkets are using
cardboard cutouts to hide the gaps

left by the supply chain
and maybe it doesn't matter if we can see

shades. Maybe my dog is looking
at the texture, or the way the clouds

smell. So easy, she licks
my tears away as we look together

at this trial-and-error horizon
of our dusking world.

*

Bye bye ,Miss American Dream

        drove resignation to the nation

in my Honda cream

        the good old girls using weed & wine

saying this will be the day that I live

        this will be the day that I live.

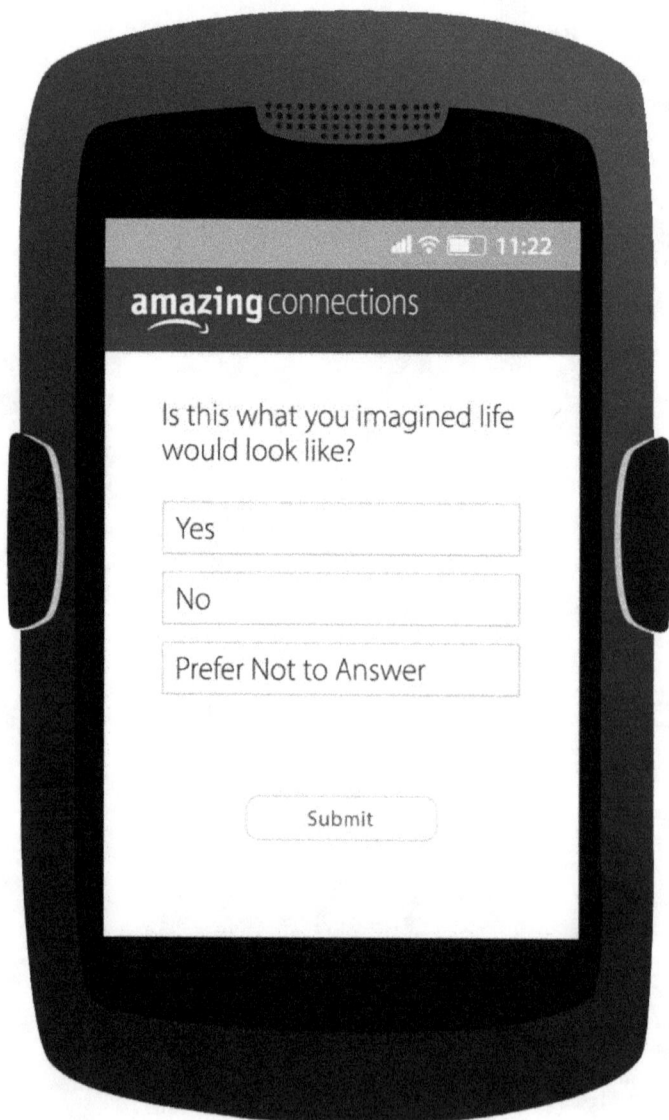

amazing connections

Is this what you imagined life would look like?

Yes

No

Prefer Not to Answer

Submit

NOTES

The letter and questionnaire was adapted from what I received from the lawyers in the mail following jury duty service. The names were redacted as well as anything that indicated more about trial specifics or lawyers.

Amazon scanners and "Roars" were written by me, designed by Ally Frame.

Crepe recipe adapted from *All Recipes*' "Basic Crepe" instructions.